HIS HOLINESS THE
DALAI LAMA

THE
little
BOOK OF
encouragement

EDITED BY RENUKA SINGH

PENGUIN
VIKING
An imprint of Penguin Random House

VIKING

USA | Canada | UK | Ireland | Australia
New Zealand | India | South Africa | China

Viking is part of the Penguin Random House group of companies
whose addresses can be found at global.penguinrandomhouse.com

Published by Penguin Random House India Pvt. Ltd
4th Floor, Capital Tower 1, MG Road,
Gurugram 122 002, Haryana, India

Penguin
Random House
India

First published in Viking by Penguin Random House India 2021

10 9 8 7 6 5 4 3 2

ISBN 9780670094943

Typeset in Sabon by Manipal Technologies Limited, Manipal
Printed at Replika Press Pvt. Ltd, India

www.penguin.co.in

MIX
Paper from
responsible sources
FSC® C016779

To my grand-nephews Sam and Harry,
and all the coming generations.

To Venerable Late Lama Thubten Yeshe and
Venerable Lama Zopa Rinpoche for their boundless
devotion to His Holiness the Fourteenth Dalai Lama.

ACKNOWLEDGEMENTS

The spread of Covid-19 has shaken up our world within a very short period. It has given rise to uncertainties, unknown fears, anxieties, loneliness, and depression. As societies and nations struggle to come to terms with and contain it, economic breakdown, migration, environmental crises, and a dwindling spirit stare us in our face. Nevertheless, it is indeed an opportune moment to explore one's interiority. His Holiness the Dalai Lama rightly points to our 'emotional hygiene' that helps the mind and heart to gain inner strength, peace, clarity, and happiness. I am grateful to His Holiness the Fourteenth Dalai Lama for being there in my life and being a reliable object of refuge for millions in this ever-changing world. His Holiness has always advocated the principle of interdependence and maintained that we are deeply connected by our humaneness which unites us all.

I am indebted to Mr Tseten Samdup Chhoekyapa from the private office of His Holiness, who generously and promptly provided sources and relevant material for this book and gave valuable suggestions and comments. Also, to Venerable Geshe Ngawang Sonam for his philosophical input and insights.

My editor Premanka Goswami encouraged and inspired me at every step to put this collection together. I would like to thank him, my other editor Ms Shreya Pandey, and the team at Penguin Random House for their hard and meticulous work.

For their patience and unfailing support, I thank my family members—Jyotsna, Sumeet, Supriti, Lisl, Sam, Harry, and the Mehtas.

I hope and pray that the 21st century will be pacific and that this book of quotations will benefit and inspire all the readers to never give up hope.

Renuka Singh
1 January 2021

FOREWORD

As one among the more than seven billion human beings alive today, I have made a commitment to promoting human happiness. We tend to think that happiness comes from money and power, without acknowledging the role of the mind or that the key to happiness is inner peace. When we are mentally distressed, physical comfort brings little relief, whereas we can often withstand physical pain if we are mentally at peace. Our modern lifestyle is focused on material goals, which are not sufficient in and of themselves to bring about inner peace. We all want to live a happy life and to do so is our right. What we need to do is to cultivate inner values such as warm-heartedness and compassion.

Similarly, whenever we face conflicts of interest, we have to think on a global level. We are interdependent. We need each other. In the globalized world in which we now live, clinging to notions of 'my nation, my faith, my community' is out of date. We need, instead, to be much more aware of the oneness of humanity, to acknowledge others' rights and interests, and on that basis, meaningful dialogue can come about.

Dr Renuka Singh, who I have known for many years, has chosen quotations concerning these topics from talks I have given in recent years and gathered them together in this book. I am very happy to have had this opportunity to share some of my thoughts and experiences with readers. If you feel anything I have said is useful, please think more about it. Discuss it with your friends and, if you can, put it into practice in day to day life.

The Dalai Lama
1 January 2021

For me, the best introduction is the human face. When I see two eyes, one mouth, one nose, I know I am dealing with another human being. I am like those young children who don't care about their companion's background, so long as they are smiling and willing to play.

Tragic situations reveal the deeper human values of compassion in us. Usually, people don't think about these deeper human values, but when they see their human brothers and sisters suffering the response comes automatically. We need a revolution of compassion that is based on warm-heartedness. This will contribute to a more compassionate world that has a sense of oneness of humanity.

Scientists have evidence to prove that basic human nature is compassionate. They have also found the opposite, that constant anger and hatred weaken our immune system. Therefore, just as we teach people physical hygiene to help preserve their physical health, for a happy and peaceful mind, we need to teach people about emotional hygiene—how to tackle their destructive emotions.

When you find that all human beings are just like you, a spirit of friendship is fostered. You find that there is less need to hide things, and as a result, feelings of fear, self-doubt, and insecurity are automatically dispelled. What's more, you earn the trust of other people!

We must recognize that we are not individuals who are alone. We depend on our community and are a part of it. No matter how rich your family is, without the community you cannot survive. In the past, there has been too much emphasis on one's continent, nation, and religion. Now that sort of thinking is considered outdated. What we really need is a sense of oneness among seven billion human beings. This could be one of the positive outcomes of the coronavirus crisis.

When we face problems, we are sometimes short-sighted and narrow-minded. Therefore, the problem appears unbearable and very big. But if we see it from a wider perspective, then it seems very small and insignificant.

There are worse places to endure a lockdown than a palace. My home, with its sweeping views of icy mountain peaks, has fresh water and pure air. I stay here peacefully. But my thoughts are with all those who are suffering and are afraid during this terrible pandemic. However, there has been much to inspire and celebrate. Many people have not cared about their safety and are helping others. It is wonderful!

As per Buddhist perspective, every sentient being is acquainted with suffering and the truths of sickness, old age, and death. But as human beings, we have the capacity to use our minds to conquer anger, panic, and greed. In recent years, I have stressed upon "emotional disarmament": seeing things realistically and clearly, without the confusion of fear or rage. If a problem has a solution, we must work to find it; if it does not, we need not waste time thinking about it.

As a Buddhist, I believe in the principle of impermanence. Eventually, this virus will pass, just as I have seen wars and other terrible threats pass in my lifetime. We will then have the opportunity to rebuild our global community as we have done many times before. I sincerely hope that everyone can stay safe and stay calm. At this time of uncertainty, it is important that we do not lose hope and confidence in the constructive efforts so many are making.

Our life depends so much on others that at the root of our existence lies a fundamental need for love. This is why it is good to cultivate an authentic sense of responsibility and concern for the welfare of others.

Sadly, the mere availability of clean drinking water is a major problem today. To prevent the uncontrolled spread of disease, we must ensure that throughout the world, the valiant health-care providers and the sick have access to the fundamental necessities of clean water and proper sanitation. Hygiene is one of the bases of effective health care.

Cultivating peace of mind should be part of our approach to health care; doctors and nurses need it too. It is important to put the patient at ease. Whenever I've gone for a medical check-up, I've noticed that I feel much more comfortable when the doctors and nurses looking after me treat me with warmth and a smile on their face. The compassionate face of a doctor is very useful.

If you would like to make me a birthday gift, the best you can do is to help fulfil my three commitments—promoting deeper human values based on the sense of oneness of humanity, encouraging harmony and understanding among the world's major religious traditions, and preserving Tibetan language and culture, the heritage Tibetans have received from the masters of India's Nalanda University, while also working for the protection of Tibet's natural environment.

Regarding my birth or of the womb's existence, I don't remember. I cannot recall if I could remember it as an infant either. However, there was one slight external sign perhaps. Children are usually born with their eyes closed; I was born with my eyes open. This may be a slight indication that I possessed a clear state of mind even in the womb.

On being recognized as the Dalai Lama, I was very happy. I liked it a lot. Even before I was recognized, I often told my mother that I was going to Lhasa. I used to straddle a windowsill in our house, pretending that I was riding a horse to Lhasa. I was a very small child at that time, but I remember this clearly. I had a strong desire to go there.

Despite my age being eighty-five years old, there's nothing wrong with my physical condition. This is mainly because my mind is at peace. I have no anxiety, and I'm inspired by these verses from Shantideva:

For as long as space endures
And as long as living beings remain
May I too abide
To dispel the misery of the world.

In order to be of service to others, not only on a physical level but also mentally, I am determined to live another fifteen to twenty years.

I am eighty-five years old. At the age of fourteen or fifteen, I lost my freedom. When I was twenty-four, I lost my country. Since 1959, Tibet has been full of suffering.

When difficult situations arise, I think carefully about Tibetans before deciding what to do, so that I have no regrets. Tibet and India have always been close, and today, India is a democratic country. So, for sixty years, I have enjoyed the freedom I have found here.

I've always considered myself to be a simple Buddhist monk; I feel that is the real me. Deep down inside, even in my dreams, I see myself as a monk. So naturally, I feel myself to be a religious person. Even in my daily life, I can say that I spend 80 per cent of my time on spiritual activities and 20 per cent on Tibet as a whole.

I switch off the light when I leave my room, take a shower instead of a bath, and eat little meat; I encourage other people to do the same. We must think globally but act locally.

*Weakness being a part
of greatness is quite a
philosophical question. It
is important to know your
weakness; then you can
improve. If some Tibetan
and Hindu Lamas consider
themselves great, it is important
to test, criticize, and tease them.
If they remain completely calm,
it shows that they truly practice
what they teach.*

We really need a sense of oneness of humanity. Thinking only of one's country, people, or religion is out of date. A lot of problems arise when our thinking is restricted to one narrow identity or another. It can lead to conflict, even wars stem from a feudal attitude. In the past, kings, queens, and sometimes even religious leaders, would go to war out of concern for their own power. They would evoke a sense of 'us' and 'them' and conscript men to fight on their behalf.

We Buddhists disapprove of killing for sport. I support those groups and people who work for animal rights and animal welfare around the world. Sadly, millions and billions of animals are killed for human consumption. What we are doing to animals today, can also happen to us. I am thinking of Tibetan butchers and Japanese fishermen; some of them ask the animals they kill for forgiveness and pray for them.

Material values do matter, but deeper inner values are more important than them. During the last century, we have made great material progress. But it is precisely this material progress that is now leading to our destruction. Material progress alone cannot reduce our psychological stress, anxiety, anger, and frustration. Scientists who once paid attention to material things are now focusing on training the mind.

Living in India, a free country, we can take advantage of the opportunity to study, and integrate what we learn into our practice. There's no point in paying lip-service to learning. Trulshik Rinpoché used to tease me, saying that the geshés may be learned, but their knowledge just amounts to empty words with no fruit. Learn through listening and reading, come to an understanding through reflection, and turn that into experience through meditation.

You must have the determination to achieve enlightenment and serve all sentient beings; we call this Bodhichitta. It is also known as 'infinite altruism'. To develop this determination, first, we must study the four noble truths. To end suffering, first, you have to know what is suffering, what is its cause? Then the cessation, and finally the path—the true path!

It is of no use to think, 'I am too old and irrelevant.' Young people are physically stronger, their minds are fresh; they can contribute to a better world, but they get over-excited. Older people have more experience; they can help by teaching and training the young. We can tell them to remain calm.

Time is always moving and is ever-changing; no force can stop that. Now the question is whether we use this time properly or not. The past cannot be changed but our future depends upon our present. We can take the opportunity to make the future happier, more peaceful, and different. So, the present generation is the key to creating a more compassionate century. They have the opportunity as well as the responsibility to do so.

I think competition is good. You trying to be at the top is not necessarily negative. If you're not trying to create problems for others and are making an effort to show them the right way, then it's good. The sense of competition is positive then. But if to reach the top, you create problems for others, that's negative.

To the young people who are protesting and are desirous of change; to those who are struggling against systems that they see as oppressive, remember—the world is always changing. Today's world is so different from what it was 100 years ago. The 20th century was a period of great violence. People readily resorted to the use of force to resolve conflict. These days, when disagreements occur, it's better to talk them through. Let's make this an era of dialogue.

Resting our hopes on the younger generation is not sufficient; politicians too must act urgently. It is not enough to hold meetings and conferences; we must set a timetable for change. Only if we start to act now will we have a reason to hope. We must not sacrifice our civilization for the greed of a few. Journalists have an equally important role. I tell them, that in these modern times, they have a special responsibility to bring awareness to the people; to not just report bad news, but bring people hope.

From the very core of our being, we simply desire contentment. I don't know whether the universe, with its countless galaxies, stars, and planets, has a deeper meaning or not, but at the very least, it is clear that we humans, who live on this earth, face the task of making a happy life for ourselves.

I feel that there is some connection between our mental state and self-confidence, and the virus. Maybe, fear gives the virus an opportunity to multiply. Otherwise, if the positive particles of the body are stronger, one may not succumb to it. Here, meditation provides an additional benefit of strengthening one's mental apparatus.

Until the late 20th century, not much attention was paid to the mind, to our mental consciousness. But towards the end of the 20th century, it began to be acknowledged that there was something else that affected our brain; meditation and breathing exercises impacted our mental consciousness. These things can help us focus on the mind itself; for a few seconds to begin with, and then, for a few minutes. I have some friends who can focus for several hours. Combining analysis with meditation enables us to achieve insight.

It's not enough to pray for one's peace of mind; one must examine what disturbs their mind and eliminate it. Likewise, just wishing to be well, won't cure our physical illness; one must take the prescribed medicine.

We are confronted with the growth of technology and artificial intelligence today. They have many helpful applications. However, since artificial intelligence is ultimately created by human intelligence, I don't envisage it taking over, as some people fear. Consciousness is not limited to sensory functions; mental consciousness is sophisticated, subtle, and powerful.

Our day-to-day existence is very much alive with hope, even though our future isn't guaranteed; there is no guarantee that tomorrow, at this time, we will be here. But still, we are working towards it purely on the basis of hope. So, we need to make the best use of our time.

Each religion has certain unique ideas or techniques and learning about them can only enrich one's faith.

Harmony among major faiths has become an essential ingredient of co-existence in our world. From this perspective, mutual understanding among these traditions is not merely the business of religious believers; it concerns the welfare of humanity as a whole.

Jesus knew about this spiritual law called 'Karma' in Buddhism and talked about it without using the word explicitly. It is a spiritual law that states you reap what you sow. Thus, everything entirely depends upon your efforts, your actions. Things change through actions and not through prayers. We must act to create positive karma; positive karma means positive action.

We should never harm each other in the name of religion. Why? Like it or not, we have to live together. The closer the contact we have with each other, the greater our admiration and appreciation of other religions will be.

I once met a physicist who told me how much he valued his field of study, but he'd also learned that he couldn't let himself become attached to it. I realized then, that although I am a Buddhist, I cannot afford to be attached to Buddhism, because that attachment can create bias and an inability to appreciate the goodness in others.

The notion of there being one truth and one religion contradicts the reality of the many truths and many religions that exist. This is clarified when we see that, as far as an individual is concerned, it's right to think of one truth and one faith; but for the larger human community, we have to acknowledge the reality that there are many truths and many faiths. This is why I always advise: keep to your religion but learn from others.

We must listen to scientists and specialists; their voices and knowledge are very important. Even religious people should pay attention to scientists, instead of just praying, praying, and praying. In the ancient Nalanda Buddhist tradition, which we Tibetans follow, everything is investigated, and not accepted by faith alone. If, through reasoning, we find some contradiction even in Buddha's own words, then we have the right to reject them.

Religion should not just be limited to praying. Ethical action is more important than prayers. What are Buddha, Allah or Christ supposed to do if we human beings destroy our earth, fill the oceans with plastic so that fish, seals and whales perish, and cause rapid desertification and vast amounts of greenhouse gases to be released into the atmosphere?

Whether one is a believer or a non-believer, one wants to live a happy life. We want friends, and friends who are smiling. If one meets angry people, one somehow wants to avoid them. A smiling person makes one feel happy. For instance, dogs sleep peacefully with their companions but avoid those dogs that are always barking. So, if one is a compassionate human being, one finds a lot of friends around.

The planet does not need more successful people; the planet desperately needs more peacemakers, healers, storytellers, and lovers of all kinds.

Good motivation and honesty bring self-confidence, which attracts the trust and respect of others. Therefore, the real source of blessings is in our own mind.

To be kind, honest and positive, to forgive those who harm us, and to treat everyone as a friend; to help those who are suffering and to never consider ourselves superior to anyone else—even if this advice seems simplistic, make the effort to see for yourself if, by following it, you can find greater happiness.

Joy and happiness are mental events, and as per our day-to-day experiences, mental satisfaction is superior to physical pleasure. We need material development, but it is a mistake to depend on material things alone to find happiness; we also need to be warm-hearted.

People face difficulties in many parts of the world; but since all seven billion of us live on this one planet, we must stand united and in solidarity with each other. When this blue planet is viewed from space, there are no national boundaries to be seen. To solely concern oneself with a nation is outdated. When affectionate relations exist between members of a family, each one is confident of being able to call on others for support. Similarly, we must constantly remind ourselves of the oneness of humanity.

*Stop grasping at some kind
of independently existing self;
you have to get rid of this
fundamental ignorance. An
understanding of the non-
inherent existence of the self,
coupled with compassion,
can destroy the fundamental
ignorance of clinging to
an independent existence.
Exchanging your happiness
with the suffering of others can
help you attain Buddhahood.*

I've been thinking about emptiness for sixty years and Bodhichitta for about fifty years. Understanding these takes time, but you have to keep analysing them. It is possible to reduce afflictive emotions. It's not easy, but if you make the effort you can, gradually, bring about a change that will give rise to peace of mind. We all have the seed of Buddhahood within us. The emptiness of Buddha's mind and that of sentient beings is the same.

Careful study, based on logic and reason, yields the understanding that things come about because of causes and conditions. Cultivating reason and logic enables the development of vast, great, profound, and swift intelligence.

Ignorance about interdependence has harmed both our natural environment and human society. We have misplaced much of our energy in self-centred material consumption, neglecting to foster the most basic and human needs of love, kindness, and cooperation. This is very sad. We have to consider what we human beings are; we are not machine-made objects. It is a mistake to seek fulfilment solely through external development.

The air we breathe, the water we drink, the forests and oceans that sustain millions of different life forms, and the climate that governs our weather systems—all transcend national boundaries. It is a sobering thought that the air we breathe contains more carbon dioxide than at any time for the past 6,50,000 years. No country, no matter how rich and powerful, or poor and weak can afford to ignore global warming.

Our environmental recklessness has brought the planet to a stage where she can no longer accept our behaviour in silence. The sheer size and frequency of environmental disasters—hurricanes, wildfires, desertification, glacial retreat, and melting of the polar ice caps—can be seen as her response to our irresponsible behaviour.

I came to Dharamsala in 1960. That winter we had a lot of snow. Later, with each passing year, the snow got less and less. We must take global warming very seriously now; I urge the world to invest more in wind and solar energy, and to move away from the dependence on fossil fuels.

Our Mother Earth is teaching us a critical and evolutionary lesson now—a lesson in universal responsibility. On this depends the survival of millions of species, including our own. The destruction of nature and natural resources stems from ignorance, greed, and a lack of respect for the earth's living things. Future generations will inherit a vastly degraded planet if destruction of the natural environment continues at the present rate.

Let us adopt a lifestyle that emphasizes contentment, because the cost of the ever-increasing standards of living is simply too great for humanity. Sometimes, we think that human beings can control nature with the help of technology; the growing emergency that rapid climate change represents now proves otherwise. We must restore the balance of nature. If we ignore this, we may soon find that all living things on this planet—including human beings—are doomed.

We are a part of nature. Nature will always be more powerful than us, despite all our knowledge, technology, and super-weapons. If the earth's average temperature increases by even two to three degrees, we will trigger a hostile climate breakdown. Morally, as beings of higher intelligence, we must care for this world and its other inhabitants. Members of the animal and plant kingdoms do not have the means to save or protect this world; it is our responsibility to undo the serious environmental degradation caused by thoughtless and inappropriate human behaviour.

The young will be at the forefront of tackling what is now one of the most pressing concerns: the need to tackle environmental challenges.
I have seen the effects of climate change in my lifetime. When I was in Tibet, I did not know about the environment; we took it for granted. We could drink water from any of the streams. It is only after I arrived in India, and later began to travel the world, that I realized how much damage was being done.

Look at the diversity of India!
All the world's major religions
flourish here, unhindered.
People in the south, north,
east and west of the country
speak different languages, have
different modes of writing, yet
they all live together as part of
the Indian Union.

During the last century, several countries have been at war with each other. I have great admiration for the spirit of the European Union though; the countries within the European Union have not waged war against another. Seventy years of peace! The European Union was rightly awarded the Nobel Peace Prize in 2012. Politics can change just as people can. The European Union is a wonderful peace project that gives me hope.

It is heartening to see that the leaders of the European Union have succeeded in meeting one of the toughest challenges in the organization's history, the pandemic, by agreeing upon a package of measures to rescue their economies from the disruption caused by it. Once again, the European Union has shown the importance of taking the common interests of all the members into account. Through persistent negotiation and compromise, the respective leaders have reached an agreement; this shows wisdom and maturity in a world often unsettled by emotional crises. I believe that the strong European Union is an inspiring model for others to follow.

Despite all the suffering that China has inflicted on Tibetans for over six decades, I remain convinced that most human conflicts can be resolved through sincere dialogue, held in the spirit of openness and reconciliation. We have learned that even enemies can become friends; I am a strong believer of non-violence.

A nuclear war between countries would probably be the last one in human history because nobody would be left to wage another war.
As to whether the world is getting better or worse, there is growing opposition to the existence of nuclear weapons.

Globally, and within individual nations, there is a huge gap between the rich and the poor. Pay more attention to the poor and try to reduce this gap. The other day, I publicly expressed the dire situation of refugees in Africa and Latin America who continue facing difficulties in their daily lives. The rich getting richer and the poor getting poorer is a very serious matter; it goes totally against our sense of compassion.

Letting go of the surplus is at the heart of spiritual growth. Just imagine what we could achieve if the USA only halved its military budget! That would be over $300 billion every year that could be used for environmental projects such as the transition to solar energy transition, or to help overcome hunger in poor countries. It would mean defending the future instead of dangerous military upgrading—the beginning of an ecological age. 'Letting go' would mean liberation.

India and China have developed a sense of competition in recent times. Both countries have populations of over a billion. Both of them are powerful nations, yet neither can destroy the other; so, they have to live side-by-side.

When you are being nationalistic, check whether the feeling is a narrow-minded, short-sighted one, which isn't so good and leads to division, or whether it is a broad-minded concern for all.

In the 21st century, I think India should show its age-old tradition of inter-religious harmony that flourishes here to the rest of the world. All the major religious traditions have lived here together in harmony for hundreds of years. Moreover, India's secular tradition of showing respect to not only all spiritual traditions but also to those who have no faith, is relevant in the context that one billion of the world's people today are agnostics.

I am just one of the seven billion human beings alive today, and as such, I try to promote human compassion based on the sense that all human beings are one. This way of thinking is of immense benefit to me. When I meet someone, with two eyes, one nose, and so forth—I recognize them as physically, mentally, and emotionally the same as me. I feel they are my sister or brother.

Many of the problems we face are created by us as a result of our narrow-mindedness and emotions. Emotions are a natural part of life, but negative emotions have no sound foundation. On the other hand, positive emotions, like compassion, are based on reason.

Among the serious problems we face today are many that we have created ourselves. In America these days, protests against racial injustice are taking place. Much of this depends on our mental attitude. We must promote a sense of oneness of humanity, which I am committed to doing. Among the seven billion human beings alive today, we're all born the same way and will all die the same way. In between these two events, while we're alive, there may be minor differences between us. But essentially, we are all the same.

Each individual must take responsibility for fighting systemic racism in modern society. Ultimately, the people, the public, have the power to decide. Firstly, people should think more wisely, with more open-mindedness. Further, the governments should take into account the public's view in our present democratic era.

Regarding mental bullying on the internet that leads young people to self-harm and suicide—as human beings, we are intelligent and can evaluate and choose what to take seriously. Even the Buddha advised his followers:

'As the wise test gold by burning, cutting and rubbing it, so bhikshus, should you accept my words only after testing them, and not merely out of respect for me.'

As a Buddhist and a follower of the Nalanda tradition, I find it very useful to always ask, 'Why?'

We Tibetans consider India our sacred neighbour because the Buddhadharma came to us from India. I jovially tell people that for thousands of years, we considered Indians our gurus, and thought of ourselves as their very reliable 'chelas' or disciples. In the guru's own land, the Nalanda tradition has seen many ups and downs. During these periods, we, as reliable chelas, have kept the Nalanda tradition intact.

*Education is another
preoccupation I have. The
whole world should pay more
attention to how they can
transform their emotions.
This should be part of one's
education and not religion.
Children need to be educated
about the inner world; we must
teach them how to develop
peace of mind.*

We are not like plants, we have emotions. We need to learn how to manage our emotions. Our education should include an understanding of how to achieve peace of mind, it should teach us how to live properly, how to balance our desire for physical comfort with that of mental comfort. We are still focusing far too much on our differences instead of our commonalities.

In our education system, we need to include lessons that focus on mental and emotional hygiene that teach people how to develop a healthy mind. This is the core of what I call secular ethics.

India's rich civilizational heritage is rooted in the long-standing traditions of karuna and ahimsa: compassion and non-violence. I believe India is the only country with the potential to combine its ancient knowledge with its modern education. We must, therefore, endeavour to integrate India's ancient wisdom with contemporary approaches to schooling, with the aim of promoting positive human values.

It is one of my commitments to revive the ancient Indian thought and tradition of ahimsa or non-violence. It is very much related to the mind, a compassionate mind, and Buddhadharma is very much a part of it. But modern Indian education is based on Western materialistic thought. India should try to synthesize ancient Indian knowledge about the mind and emotion with modern education.

It is my wish that more attention is paid to educating the heart—teaching love, kindness, peace, compassion, forgiveness, mindfulness, self-discipline, generosity, and tolerance. This education is necessary from kindergarten to secondary schools, and even in universities. I am alluding to social-emotional and ethical learning. We need a worldwide initiative for educating the heart and training the mind in this modern age.

*We in Tibet have preserved
the knowledge and cultural
heritage which has come to
us from India over a period
of thousand years. Being
a student of logic, I find it
very useful. Even Buddha
himself expressed, 'Oh! My
follower, you should not
accept my teaching out of
faith or devotion but rather
through thorough investigation
and experiment.' If we find
something unconvincing,
we must reject it. This is
quite unique to the Tibetan
knowledge-system.*

*Hours, minutes, and seconds—
time never stands still. We too
are a part of nature. The past
is important, but already past.
The future is still in our hands,
so we must think about ecology
at the global level.*

I am an ardent supporter of environmental protection. We humans are the only species with the power to destroy the earth as we know it. Yet, if we have the capacity to destroy the earth, so too we have the capacity to protect it. We must ethically re-examine what we have inherited, what we are responsible for, and what we will pass on to the coming generations.

Environmental education about the consequences of the destruction of our ecosystem and the dramatic decrease in biodiversity must be given top priority. However, creating awareness is not sufficient; we must find ways to bring about changes in the way we live. I call on the younger generation—be rebels! Demand climate protection and justice because it is your future that is at stake.

Today, the pandemic is one threat we face. Another very serious issue is that of climate change and global warming. Scientists have predicted that if we don't act to stop it now, in the coming decades, water sources like rivers and lakes, may dry up. An additional problem that needs to be addressed is that of the growing gap between the rich and the poor. Tackling these difficult circumstances will require that we work together.

Buddha would be green, and I am green too. Buddha was born as his mother leaned against a tree for support. He attained enlightenment seated beneath a tree and passed away as trees stood witness overhead. Therefore, was Buddha to return to our world, he would certainly be connected to the campaign to protect the environment.

If we compare the damage done to the environment due to war and violence, it becomes clear that the violence has had an immediate impact on us. The trouble is that the damage done to the environment takes place more stealthily, so we don't see it until it is too late. We have reached a tipping point when it comes to global warming.

*Any human activity should
be carried out with a sense of
responsibility, commitment,
and discipline. But if our
activities are carried out with
short-sightedness and for short-
term gains of money or power,
then they all become negative
and destructive activities.*

Human beings are physically, mentally, and emotionally the same. Everybody wants to live a happy life, free of problems. Even insects, birds, and animals want to be happy. To ensure a more peaceful world and a healthier environment, we sometimes point a finger at others, saying they should do this or that; but change must start with us, as individuals.

The metaphysics of the wise men of ancient India and the West are converging in times of ecological crisis. Technology alone will not save us. We need interdependence in terms of ethics and technology. We need a joint plan to save the planet.

According to scientists, basic human nature is compassionate. Those who grow up in a more compassionate atmosphere tend to be happier and more successful. On the other hand, scientists suggest that living with constant anger or fear undermines our immune system. Hence, compassion and warm-heartedness are not only important at the beginning of our life but also towards the middle and at the end of it.

The Tibetan plateau happens to be the largest water tank in the world. All the major rivers of Asia—including the Ganges, Karnali, Brahmaputra, Indus, Sutlej, Irrawaddy, Salween, Yellow River, Yangtse, and the Mekong—originate in the Tibetan plateau. Over 1.5 billion people live by these waters: one-fifth of the world's population. Without water, there is no life. If Tibet's 46,000 glaciers continue to melt, we will face unimaginable water problems, and water will probably become a key cause for conflict in the future.

New technology has always taken a relatively long time to make a complete breakthrough. More and more companies are making electric cars. But if the cost of the car is too expensive, then only the rich will be able to buy them. So, these cars must be made more affordable. Similarly, other forms of renewable energy must be made more affordable, especially to the poorer sections of the community who are the most vulnerable.

One of my dreams, perhaps an impossible dream, is to harness the solar potential of places like the Sahara Desert and to use the power to run desalination plants. The sweet water thus produced could nurture the desert and produce food crops. It is a project that would have widespread benefits and would function on a scale that requires global cooperation.

As a Buddhist monk who believes in rebirth, I say—even for selfish reasons, we must pay more attention to our planet. Because we will come back. And all of us would like to live on a healthy earth. The belief in rebirth calls for more protection of our environment and climate.

In keeping with the Tibetan Buddhist tradition: all sentient beings have been our mothers. The entire Buddhist spirituality is characterized by this realization. All sentient beings are connected by a maternal bond. This is the basic truth of awakening, enlightenment, and realization. We are all interconnected in the universe, and from this, universal responsibility arises.

Being too self-centred can give rise to anxiety and depression. An effective antidote is to cultivate a sense of altruism, taking the whole of humanity into account.

Only when we understand that the earth is like our mother—mother earth, will we take care of her. We Tibetans, like the ancient people of India, understand this interdependence. A healthy earth means healthy animals, healthy plants, healthy forests, healthy water, and healthy people. Mother earth warns us today, 'My children are behaving badly.' She is warning us that there are limits to our actions.

When you spend time in the forest and hear birds singing, you feel good inside. The healing power of forests is becoming increasingly important. When we are surrounded by artificial things, it is harder to be at peace. It's as if we become artificial ourselves; we develop hypocrisy, suspicion, and distrust. In that state, it's hard to develop a genuine, warm-hearted friendship. We all feel the need to be surrounded by life. We need life around us that grows, flourishes, and thrives.

What I find particularly worrying is intensive animal husbandry. We humans can, largely, live with little to no meat, and above all, without animals suffering. Particularly in the modern world, we have many alternatives— especially fruits and vegetables. There is even meat being made from vegetables like peas, beetroot, potatoes, and coconuts. Intensive animal husbandry has serious consequences, not only for animals but also for man's health, the soil, the insects, and the air.

It is my vision to make my home country, Tibet, into the world's largest nature preserve. Following the ancient Tibetan Buddhist tradition, Tibet must and can become a demilitarized sanctuary of peace and nature.

*Look at bees. They have no
constitution, police forces,
or moral training, but they
work together to survive.
Though they may occasionally
squabble, the colony survives
due to cooperation. Human
beings, whereas, have
constitutions, complex legal
systems, and police forces. We
have remarkable intelligence
and a great capacity for love
and affection; yet, despite our
many extraordinary qualities,
we seem less able to cooperate.*

Fear and anxiety easily give way to anger and violence. The opposite of fear is trust, which is related to warm-heartedness and boosts our self-confidence. Compassion also reduces fear, reflecting as it does a concern for others' well-being. When we are under the sway of anger or attachment, we are limited in our ability to take a full and realistic view of the situation. When the mind is compassionate, it is calm and we are able to use our sense of reason practically, realistically, and with determination.

Time passes, things change; so, we need to find new ways of thinking. You young people are the ones who will contribute to the making of a new world. Don't fall into the old ways of thinking! Accept the new reality about the oneness of all human beings and face up to the challenge of global warming. Open your eyes and open your minds.

*In the Tibetan tradition, in
terms of coping with adversity,
victims are encouraged
to cultivate forbearance.
The first stage of that is to
develop a sense of equanimity.
Forbearance builds up resilience
and protects you from giving
in to disturbing emotional
impulses.*

We human beings have these marvellous, brilliant minds. But we are also the biggest troublemakers on the planet. We should utilize our brains with compassion and a sense of concern.

What is important is not how long you live, but whether you live a meaningful life. This doesn't mean accumulating money and fame but being of service to your fellow human beings. It means helping others if you can; but even if you can't, at least do not harm them.

We have this unique human intelligence. We should use it to solve the challenges we face, and never give up or tell ourselves there's no hope. If you have a positive goal and you're well-motivated to seek the well-being of others, no matter how difficult it is to achieve, you must remain determined.

The very purpose of my life is to serve as much as I can.

Until the age of thirteen, I had no interest in studying; I was only interested in playing. So, my tutor would show me the holy whip occasionally, not with the intention of inflicting violence, but out of sincere motivation to train me. Sometimes this method is effective in disciplining the student.

Even though I was the Dalai Lama, I had thirteen years of study as an ordinary student before becoming a refugee. I continuously studied these 300 volumes of translations from India. Even these days, I am always going through these books. Today we have preserved this knowledge in monastic institutions in South India. There are around 10,000 monks who attend the course for at least twenty years. Along with this, in the nunnery, the nuns can also obtain a PhD. Initially, some people had reservations about this. But you see, Buddha

*gave virtually the same rank
to nuns and monks, so I felt
they should also have an equal
opportunity to study.*

I've always believed that one's mother is one's first teacher, and she teaches compassion. The day after my birth, I experienced my mother's compassion. This is, I think, the most important part of building a healthy family, which in turn leads to a healthy humanity.

My village was very small, and of course, there were no toys; so my mother always carried me wherever she went, especially to the farm for work. Eventually, I felt very comfortable being on my mother's shoulder. Then I become a little bolder and instructed my mother to take me to see some gorgeous sights. She was a bit too kind, and I was the boy who was a little bit spoiled.

The mother is a symbol of love and kindness. So, a woman should not only be concerned about the family but society as well.

No matter how difficult the situation may be, we should employ science and human ingenuity with determination and courage to overcome the problems that confront us. Faced with threats to our health and well-being, it is natural to feel anxious and afraid. Everyone, at present, is doing their best to contain the spread of the coronavirus. I applaud the concerted efforts of nations to limit the threat.

Suffering caused by diseases, ageing, hunger, or loneliness, can be found throughout the world. We encounter life's difficulties daily. There is also much to appreciate—the kindness and mutual support shown by so many members of our human family. And then, there are the opportunities life provides to serve and act in a selfless, generous, and patient manner towards our brothers and sisters.

At the root of human suffering is our excessive self-centredness, a fixation on our own needs rather than the greater good. In contrast, feelings of compassion, empathy, love, and kindness shift our focus outwards—restoring us to happiness.

Individuals who cultivate peace of mind lead to a more peaceful society, and that in turn contributes to a more peaceful world. All beings want to find joy; we depend on hope, which is the pursuit of something good. But to do that we need to use our brains properly. Real happiness depends not on sensory awareness, but on the mind itself; the key is to establish peace of mind. Doing that requires that we understand the mind's system and our emotions, something that was thoroughly examined in ancient India.

Buddhist teachers remind us that each of us is a student and everyone else in the world is our teacher; that those who cause us the most difficulty can be the best teachers, and it is towards them we would be wise to feel a sense of gratitude. We must learn to appreciate the opportunity they provide and develop compassion towards them. Our compassion must contain the ability to listen with an open mind.

I have always been fascinated by the experimental and empirical pursuit of knowledge known as science. When I was young, I enjoyed taking apart mechanical toys and putting them back together. Had I not been chosen at a young age to be the 14th Dalai Lama of Tibet, I would have probably become an engineer or electrician. For more than thirty years, I have spent much time with Western scientists. When I think about myself now, I sometimes think I am only one-half a Buddhist monk—the other half being a scientist.

It is encouraging to see so many ordinary people across the world displaying great compassion toward the plight of refugees—from those who have rescued them from the sea to those who have taken them in and provided friendship and support. As a refugee myself, I feel a strong empathy towards fellow refugees. When we see their anguish, we should do all we can to help them.

These days I watch one to two hours of television, read sometimes, and then meditate daily for four to five hours. It is very helpful. Watching videos of animals is very relaxing. Sometimes tigers and leopards make me uncomfortable, but deer and similar animals are very peaceful. When you look at animals, you can really appreciate your human life. Doing an early morning meditation is useful for people who are isolated, anxious, and adjusting to life around a global pandemic and its restrictions. Even if you start with one-second meditations, work your way up to one minute, then five, ten . . . and be compassionate.

Every morning, when I wake up, I try to reflect on the question of, 'Who am I?' When you search for the identity of the 'I' you cannot find anything that you can point your finger at. However, the 'I' or the self does exist. We tend to develop this inappropriate thinking of an independent 'I', based on which all the destructive emotions arise. This is a fundamental ignorance, a belief in an independently existing, concrete 'I', which is non-existent.

I have always opposed the objectification of women, have supported women and their rights, and celebrated the growing international consensus in support of gender equality and respect for women. I have encouraged Tibetan nuns in exile to pursue a high level of scholarship, previously reserved only for male monks. I have frequently suggested that if we had more women leaders, the world would be a more peaceful place.

I always tell Tibetans: it is much better to consider the Chinese as our brothers and sisters than to think of them as our enemy—no use in that. For the time being, there is a problem with our Chinese neighbours, but only with a few individuals in the Communist Party. A number of Chinese leaders now realize that their seventy-year-old policy regarding Tibet is unrealistic. There was too much emphasis on the use of force then. So now they are in a dilemma: how to deal with the Tibetan problem? Things seem to be changing.

I cannot say I am the incarnation of the bodhisattva of infinite compassion, Avalokiteshvara, unless I am engaged in a meditative effort, such as that of following my life back, breath by breath.

There are four types of rebirth. First, the common type, wherein a being is helpless to determine his or her rebirth and depends on the nature of his past actions. Second, the opposite—the birth of an entirely enlightened Buddha, who simply manifests a physical form to help others. Third, the birth of one who, due to past spiritual attainments, can choose, or at least influence, the place and situation of his rebirth. And the fourth, known as the 'blessed manifestation'. In this, the person is blessed beyond his normal capacity to perform helpful functions. To attain this last type of birth, the person's desire to help people in his previous lives must have been very strong.

I have the karmic relationship to be in the role of the Dalai Lama. I am at home with it. You may consider that, under the circumstances, I am very lucky. However, behind the word 'luck', there are actual causes or reasons. There is the karmic force of my ability to assume this role as well as the force of my wish to do so. Part of my daily prayer is this:

> *'As long as space exists, and as long as there are migrators in cyclic existence, may I remain to remove their sufferings.'*

I have wished for it in this lifetime, and I know I'd wished for this in my previous lifetimes.

My death may well mark the end of the great tradition of Dalai Lamas; the word means 'great leader' in Tibetan. It may end with this great Lama. The Himalayan Buddhists of Tibet and Mongolia will decide what happens next. They will determine whether the 14th Dalai Lama has been reincarnated in another tulku. What my followers decide is not an issue for me; I have no interest. My only hope is that when my last days come, I will still have my good name and will feel that I have made some contribution to humanity.

In this time of serious crisis, we face threats to our health, and feel sadness for the family and friends we have lost. Economic disruption is posing a major challenge to governments and undermining the ability of so many people to make a living. The crisis and its consequences serve as a warning—only by coming together in a coordinated global response, will we meet the unprecedented magnitude of the challenges we face. I pray we all heed the call to unite.

ABOUT THE AUTHOR

TENZIN GYATSO, His Holiness the fourteenth Dalai Lama of Tibet, is the spiritual leader of Tibetan Buddhists and a Nobel laureate. In 1950, at the age of fifteen, he was called upon to assume full responsibility as Head of State and Government. His efforts to bring about a peaceful solution to the Sino-Tibetan problem were thwarted and, following the suppression of the 10 March 1959 Tibetan national uprising, His Holiness escaped to India where he was given political asylum. In exile, he has successfully led his people in the field of education, rehabilitation, and preservation of the ancient and unique Tibetan culture. He is also recognized as an advocate of world peace and inter-religious understanding. His Holiness has written several books on Buddhism, philosophy, human nature, and universal responsibility. He has received many international awards, including the 1989 Nobel Peace Prize.

RENUKA SINGH, former Professor and Sociologist from the Centre for the Study of Social Systems, Jawaharlal Nehru University, New Delhi, has been working in the field of Gender Studies, Diaspora, and Buddhist Studies for over four decades. She has been associated with Women's Studies Centre, Delhi University, Centre for Social Research, and was a Research Fellow at Centre for Cross-Cultural Research on Women at Oxford University, UK. She was also a Senior UGC Fellow and is currently the Director of Tushita Mahayana Meditation Centre, New Delhi. She has authored and edited several articles and books that have been translated into several languages of the world.

MORE FROM THE AUTHOR

Daily Inspirations

Courage, compassion, wisdom, and inspiration for everyday
from His Holiness the Dalai Lama

Chronologically arranged for each calendar day, this book
offers words of wisdom and motivation to deal with the
challenges of life.